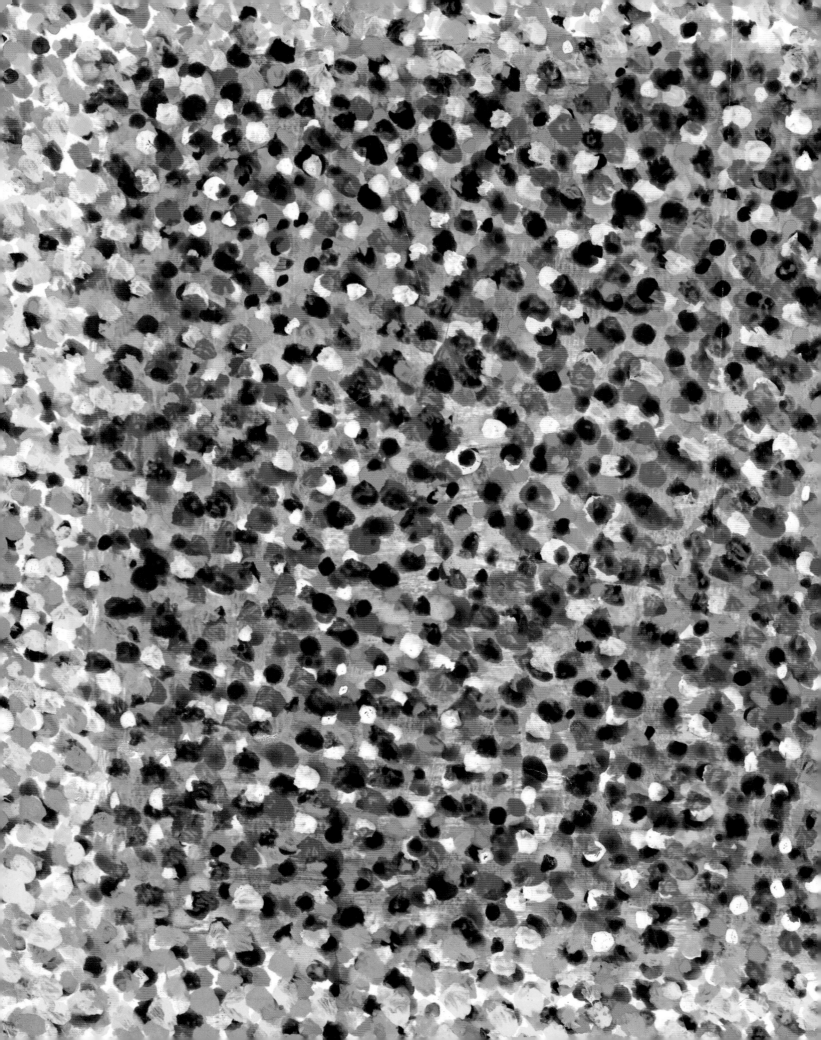

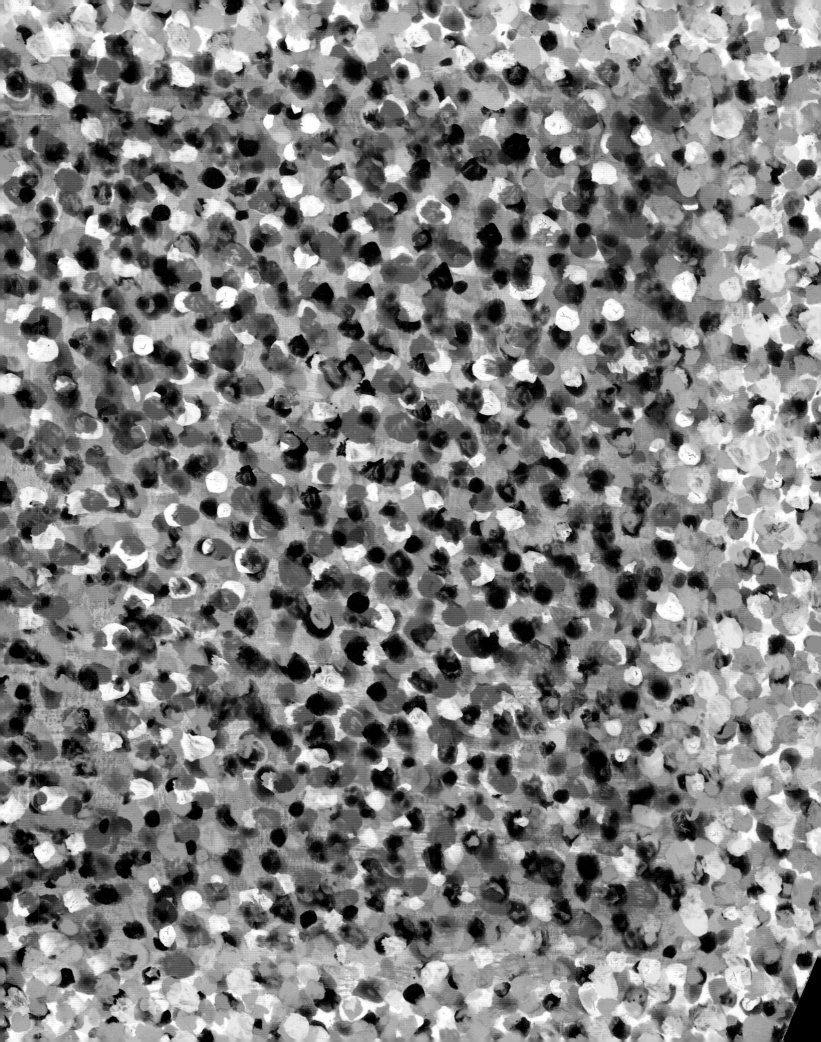

For Martha & Leighton

Eric Carle's ANIMALS ANIMALS

world of
ERiC CARLE™

There is only one horse on all the earth
and his name is All Horses.
There is only one bird in the air
and his name is All Wings.
There is only one fish in the seas
and his name is All Fins.
There is only one man in all the world
and his name is All Men.
There is only one woman in all the world
and her name is All Women.
There is only one child in the world
and the child's name is All Children.

There is only one Maker in all the world
and His children cover the earth,
and they are named All God's Children.

Carl Sandburg

And God created great whales, and every living creature that moveth, which the waters brought forth abundantly after their kind . . .

Bible, Genesis

I throw myself to the left.
I turn myself to the right.
I am the fish
Who glides in the water, who glides,
Who twists himself, who leaps.
Everything lives, everything dances, everything sings.

African Pygmy

Leaping flying fish!
Dancing for me and my
                boat
as I sail for home.

Haiku, Koson

11

Butterflies dancing through falling snow!
What a wonderful sight it would be!

Haiku, Demaru

How sadly the bird in his cage
Watches the butterflies.

Haiku, Issa

The Octopus

Tell me, O Octopus, I begs,
Is those things arms or is they legs?
I marvel at thee, Octopus;
If I were thou, I'd call me Us.

Ogden Nash

Sea Turtle

Paddling, we saw that turtle; saw its eyes open,
 its flippers outstretched, as it floated
Seawater lapped at its shell, spreading across its back.

Australian Aborigine

Bat

Dark air-life looping
Yet missing the pure loop . . .
A twitch, a twitter, an elastic shudder in flight
And serrated wings against the sky,
like a glove, a black glove thrown up at the light,
And falling back.

D. H. Lawrence

Every Insect

Every Insect (ant, fly, bee)
Is divided into three:
One head, one chest, one stomach part.

Some have brains.
All have a heart.

Insects have no bones,

No noses.

But with feelers they can smell
Dinner half a mile away.

Can your nose do half as well?

Also you'd be in a fix
With all those legs to manage:
Six.

Dorothy Aldis

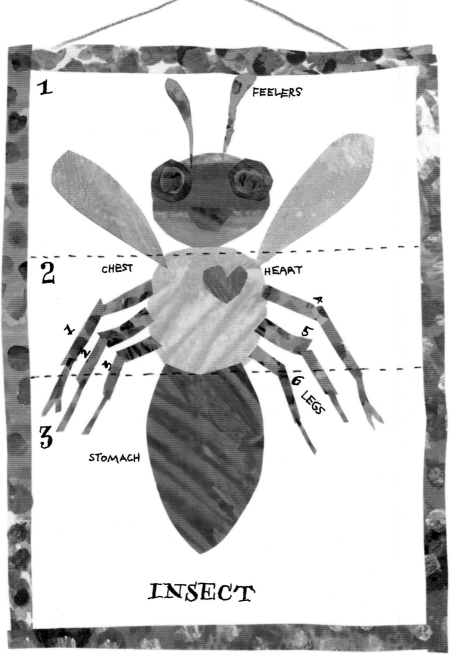

The Ant

The ant is knowing and wise; but
he doesn't know enough to take a vacation.

Clarence Day

Crickets

We cannot say that crickets sing
Since all they do is twang a wing.

Especially when the wind is still
They orchestrate a sunlit hill.

And in the evening blue above
They weave the stars and moon with love.

Then peacefully they chirp all night
Remembering delight, delight . . .

Harry Behn

Bee! I'm Expecting You

Bee! I'm expecting you!
Was saying Yesterday
To Somebody you know
That you were due—

The Frogs got Home last Week—
And settled, and at work—
Birds, mostly back—
The Clover warm and thick—

You'll get my Letter by
The seventeenth; Reply,
Or better, be with me—
Yours, Fly.

Emily Dickinson

My Opinion

Is a caterpillar ticklish?
   Well, it's always my belief
That he giggles as he wiggles
   Across a hairy leaf.

Monica Shannon

M was once a little mouse.
       Mousy,
       Bousy,
       Sousy,
       Mousy.
In the housy,
       Little mouse!

Edward Lear

The Birthday Cow

Happy Mooday to you,
Happy Mooday to you.
Happy Mooday,
Dear Yooday.
Happy Mooday to you.

Eve Merriam

Baby Chick

Peck
  peck
    peck
on the warm brown egg.
OUT comes a neck.
OUT comes a leg.

How
  does
    a chick
who's not been about,
discover the trick
of how to get out?

Aileen Fisher

Commissariat Camels

We haven't a camelty tune of our own
To help us trollop along.
But every neck is a hairy trombone,
Rtt-ta-ta-ta! is a hairy trombone.
And this is our marching song:
Can't! Don't! Shan't! Won't!
Pass it along the line!

Rudyard Kipling

The bear stands.
I am telling you this.
Yonder the bear stands.
He faces the east just before the sun appears.
Yonder the bear stands.
Now the sun is coming.

Pawnee Indian

The tail of a fox will show no matter how hard he tries to hide it.

Hungarian proverb

The Duck-Billed Platypus

The duck-billed platypus isn't easy to imagine,
of all the earthly creatures he is most unique,
lays eggs like a bird but suckles like an animal,
and swims like a fish at the bottom of a creek.

If you ask it why it behaves so confusingly,
It hides in a hole and simply will not speak,
All that I can say, it's a shy individual,
An oddity of nature and a very charming freak!

Arnold Sundgaard

A Cat May Look at a King

The Cat
    Came and sat
    Down before His Majesty.
The Cat
Came and sat
Down before the King.
"I've come to take a look.
For unless I am mistook,
It is written in this book,
I may do this thing!"

She took
Quite a look.
    Over all His Majesty.
She took
Quite a look
    And then she shook her head.
"There's little here to praise.
Plain his looks and dull his ways;
I'll turn my loving gaze
On Tabby Tom instead!"

Laura Richards

A handful does not satisfy a lion.

Talmud

The Elephant

The elephant is quite a beast,
He's rather large to say the least,
And though his size is most impressive
The elephant is not aggressive,
He never throws his weight around,
Still he always holds his ground.
He only wants to feel secure.
Long may the elephant endure!

Arnold Sundgaard

Travel Plans

If I could go anywhere,
      Here's what I'd do.
I'd pop in the pouch of a kind
      kangaroo.
I'd travel around for as long
      as I pleased,
And learn to say "thank you"
      in Kangarooese.

Bobbi Katz

Seal Lullaby

Oh! hush thee, my baby, the night is behind us.
    And black are the waters that sparkled so green.
The moon, o'er the combers, looks downward to find us
    At rest in the hollows that rustle between.
Where billow meets billow, there soft be thy pillow;
    Ah, weary wee flipperling, curl at thy ease!
The storm shall not wake thee, no shark overtake thee.
    Asleep in the arms of the slow-swinging seas.

Rudyard Kipling

The Tortoise and the Hedgehog

Can't curl, but can swim—
Slow-Solid, that's him!
Curls up, but can't swim—
Stickly-Prickly, that's him.

Rudyard Kipling

Busy

Busy, busy, busy, busy,
Busy little squirrel—
Running, running, jumping,
In a dizzy whirl.
Stopping now and then to eat
A tasty little acorn treat—
Busy, busy, busy, busy,
Busy little squirrel.

Phyllis Halloran

Butterfly

What is a butterfly? At best
He's but a caterpillar dressed.

Benjamin Franklin

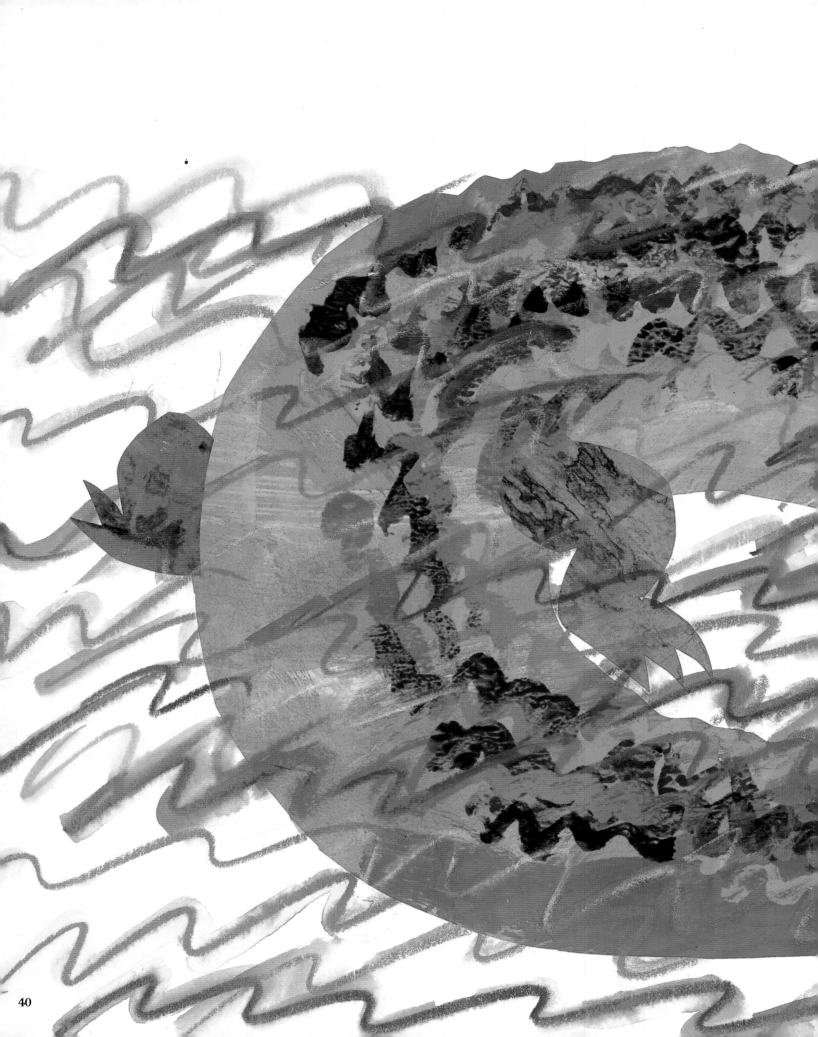

How Doth the Little Crocodile

How doth the little crocodile
  Improve his shining tail,
And pour the waters of the Nile
  On every golden scale!

How cheerfully he seems to grin,
  How neatly spreads his claws,
And welcomes little fishes in,
  With greatly smiling jaws!

Lewis Carroll

The Duck

Behold the duck.
It does not cluck.
A cluck it lacks.
It quacks.
It is especially fond
Of a puddle or pond.
When it dines or sups,
It bottoms up.

Ogden Nash

Long Gone

Don't waste your time in looking for
the long-extinct tyrannosaur,
because this ancient dinosaur
just can't be found here anymore.

This also goes for stegosaurus,
allosaurus, brontosaurus
and any other kind of saurus.
They all lived here before us.

Jack Prelutsky

The Lizard

The Lizard is a timid thing
That cannot dance or fly or sing;
He hunts for bugs beneath the floor
And longs to be a dinosaur.

John Gardner

Five little owls in the old elm tree
Fluffy and puffy as owls could be,
Blinking and winking with big round eyes
At the big round moon that hung in the skies.
As I passed beneath, I could hear one say,
"There'll be mouse for supper, there will today."
Then all of them hooted "Tu-whit, Tu-whoo!
Yes, mouse for supper, Hoo hoo. Hoo hoo!"

Anonymous

Firefly

A little light is going by,
Is going up to see the sky,
A little light with wings.

I never could have thought of it,
To have a little bug all lit
And made to go on wings.

Elizabeth Madox Roberts

Giraffes

Giraffes
I like them.
Ask me why.
Because they hold their heads up high.
Because their necks stretch to the sky.
Because they're quiet, calm, and shy.
Because they run so fast they fly,
Because their eyes are velvet brown.
Because their coats are spotted tan.
Because they eat the tops of trees.
Because their legs have knobby knees.
Because
Because
Because. That's why
I like giraffes.

Mary Ann Hoberman

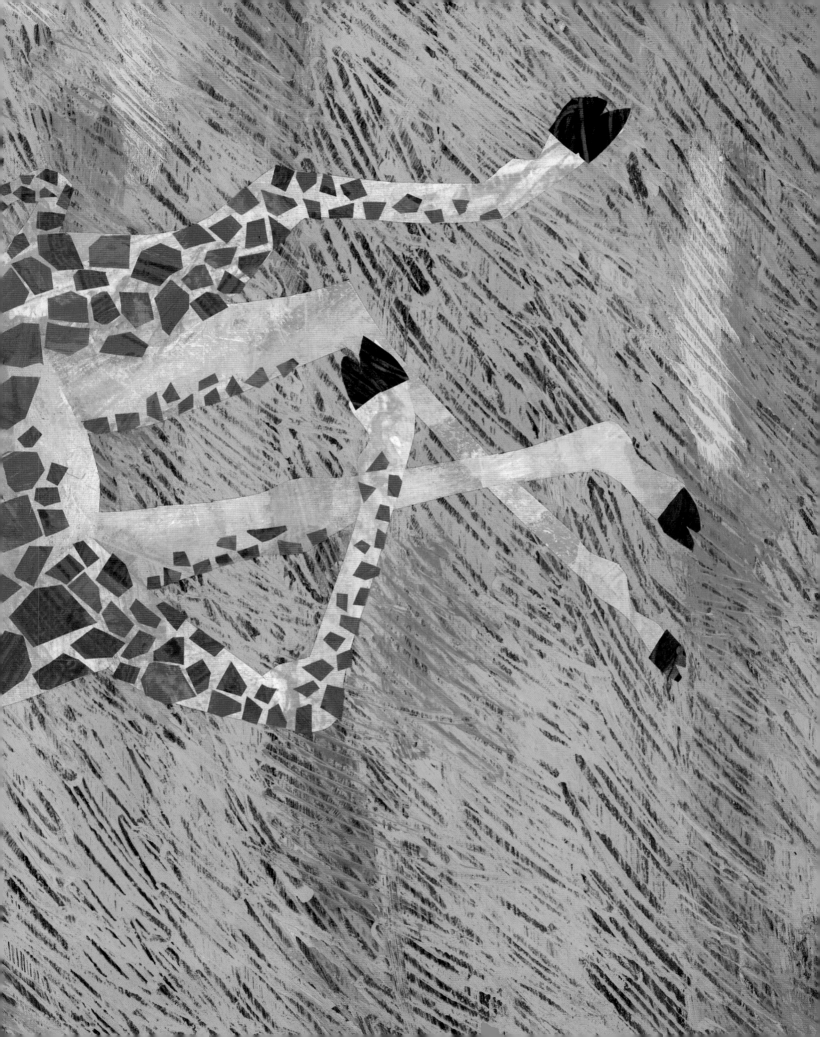

"Quack!" Said the Billy Goat

"Quack!" said the billy goat,
    "Oink!" said the hen.
"Miaow!" said the little chick
    Running in the pen.

"Hobble-gobble!" said the dog,
    "Cluck!" said the sow.
"Tu-whit-tu-whoo!" the donkey said,
    "Baa!" said the cow.

"Hee-haw!" the turkey cried,
    The duck began to moo.
All at once the sheep went,
    "Cock-a-doodle-doo!"
"Bleat! Bleat!" said the owl
    When he began to speak.
"Bow-wow!" said the cock
    Swimming in the creek.

"Cheep-cheep!" said the cat
    As she began to fly.
"Farmer's been and laid an egg—
    That's the reason why."

Charles Causley

If a rooster crows when he goes to bed
He'll get up with rain on his head.

Weather saying

When a peacock loudly calls
Then look out for rain and squalls.

Weather saying

What fun   to be
A Hippo   -potamus
And weigh   a ton
From top   to bottamus.

Michael Flanders

The Porcupine

A porcupine looks somewhat silly.
He also is extremely quilly.
And if he shoots a quill at you,
Run fast
Or you'll be quilly too.

I would not want a porcupine
To be my loving valentine.

Karla Kuskin

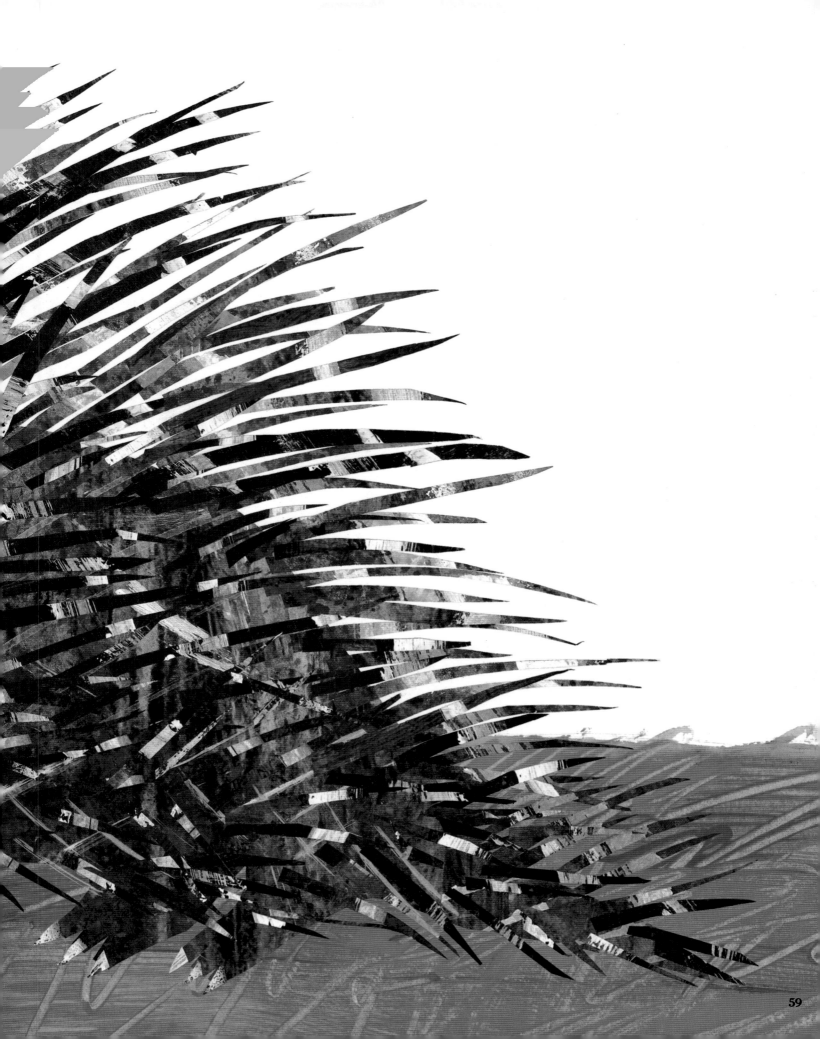

Mother Doesn't Want a Dog

Mother doesn't want a dog.
Mother says they smell,
And never sit when you say sit
Or even when you yell.
And when you come home late at night,
And there is ice and snow,
You have to go back out because
The dumb dog has to go.

Mother doesn't want a dog.
Mother says they shed,
And always let the strangers in
And bark at friends instead.
And do disgraceful things on rugs,
And track mud on the floor,
And flop upon your bed at night
And snore their doggy snore.

Mother doesn't want a dog.
She's making a mistake.
Because, more than a dog, I think
She will not want this snake.

Judith Viorst

The Flying Squirrel

The Flying Squirrel is crazy.
Though he has no feathers (much less wings),
He scampers up into the tallest tree
And cries, "Toot-toot! I'm a parachute!"
And away off the highest branches he springs
Into empty air, spreading every hair,
His arms and legs spread wide to the side,
Till he lands with a thump that's almost quiet . . .

Admire it child, but don't try it.

John Gardner

The Bird's Nest

I know a place, in the ivy on a tree,
Where a bird's nest is, and the eggs are three,
And the bird is brown, and the eggs are blue,
And the twigs are old, but the moss is new,
And I go quite near, though I think I should have heard
The sound of me watching, if I had been a bird.

John Drinkwater

Narwhal

Around their igloo fires with glee
   The Eskimos tell tales
Of Narwhal. Listen and you'll see
   This unicorn of whales
Through frosty waves off Greenland's
          coast
   Majestically advance.
And like a knight come forth
     to joust
   Hold high its ivory lance.

X. J. Kennedy

Enigma Sartorial

Consider the Penguin.
He's smart as can be—
Dressed in his dinner clothes
Permanently.
You never can tell
When you see him about,
If he's just coming in
Or just going out!

Lucy W. Rhu

Yak

Yickity-yackity, yickity-yak,
the yak has a scriffily, scraffily back,
some yaks are brown yaks and some yaks are black,
yickity-yackity, yickity-yak.

Sniggildy-snaggildy, sniggildy-snag,
the yak is all covered with shiggildy-shag;
he walks with a ziggildy-zaggildy-zag,
sniggildy-snaggildy, sniggildy-snag.

Jack Prelutsky

The Pelican Chorus

King and Queen of the Pelicans we;
   No other birds so grand we see!
None but we have feet like fins!
With lovely, leathery throats and chins!
      Ploffskin, Pluffskin, Pelican jee!
      We think no birds as happy as we!
      Plumpskin, Plashkin, Pelican jill!
      We think so then, and we thought so still!

Edward Lear

Sparrow

A hummingbird hums.

A jay finds fighting
Pretty exciting
And licks every bird in sight.

A woodpecker drums.

A swallow swoops
In up-and-down loops
And seldom lights on the ground.

A gull is graceful in flight.

But take a sparrow
Whose world is narrow,
A sparrow just hangs around.

And an owl hoo-hoos
Whenever it gives a hoot.

A partridge whirs
Through the pines and the firs.

A chickadee's ways are cute.

A crow steals corn
From the year it's born
Then hides where it can't be found.

A sparrow, though,
Doesn't come and go,
A sparrow just hangs around.

Kaye Starbird

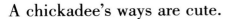
A pigeon coos

The Eagle

The sun's rays
Lie along my wings
And stretch beyond their tips.

Papago Indian

I will not change my horse with any that treads . . .
When I bestride him I soar. I am a hawk.
He trots the air; the earth sings when he touches it.

Shakespeare

Galloping pony—
alone, against the moonlight,
on a whitened beach.

Haiku, Kyorai

Tiger

The tiger
has swallowed
a black sun.

In his cold
cage he
carries it still.

Black flames
flicker through
his fur.

Black rays roar
from the centers
of his eyes.

Valerie Worth

The Barracuda

Slowly, slowly he cruises,
And slowly, slowly he chooses
Which kind of fish he prefers to take this morning;
Then without warning
The Barracuda opens his jaws, teeth flashing,
And with a horrible, horrible grinding and gnashing,
Devours a hundred poor creatures and feels no remorse.
It's no wonder of course,
That he really ought, perhaps, to change his ways.
"But" (as he says
With an evil grin)
"It's actually not my fault, you see!
I've nothing to do with the tragedy;
I open my mouth for a yawn and—ah me—
They all
         swim
            in."

John Gardner

Electric Eel

Some think Electric Eel lacks looks,
Some others find it stunning.
A homegrown battery it packs
To keep its shocker running.

Why, you could light all New York's streets
And sky scrapers and stuff,
With one Electric Eel alone
If it were long enough.

X. J. Kennedy

The face of the dragonfly
Is practically nothing
        But eyes.

Haiku, Chisoku

A discovery!
On my frog's smooth green belly
there sits no button.

Haiku, Yaku

Snail

Snail upon the wall,
Have you got at all
Anything to tell
About your shell?

Only this, my child—
When the wind is wild,
Or when the sun is hot,
It's all I've got.

John Drinkwater

Roosters

"Get out of my way!"
   says Rooster One.
"I won't!"
   says Rooster Two.
"You won't?"
"I won't!"
"You shall!"
"I shan't!"
Cock cock-a-
doodle-doo.
They picked.
They kicked.
They fought for hours.
There was a great
to-do!
"You're a very fine fighter,"
   says Rooster One.
"You're right!"
   says Rooster Two.

Elizabeth Coatsworth

The Red Hen

She turned her head to this side;
　　She turned her head to that.
Looking round for tidbits,
　　Juicy ones and fat.

Scritchy-scratch went Red Hen's feet;
　　Nib-nob went her bill.
She ate of juicy tidbits,
　　Until she had her fill.

And then she flew into a nest
　　And laid an egg, and then.
With a cut-cut-cut, ca-dah-cut,
　　Flew off to eat again.

James S. Tippett

Rhinoceros

I often wonder whether
The rhinoceros's leather
Is as bumpy on the inside
As it is upon the skinside.

Mary Ann Hoberman

Hurt no living thing:
  Ladybird, nor butterfly,
Nor moth with dusty wing,
  Nor cricket chirping cheerily,
Nor grasshopper so light of leap.
  Nor dancing gnat, or beetle flat,
Nor harmless worms that creep.

Christina Rossetti

Index of Animals Alphabetically Arranged

Index of First Lines

Elizabeth Madox Roberts: "Firefly," by Elizabeth Madox Roberts, from *Under the Tree*, by Elizabeth Madox Roberts. Copyright © 1922 by B. W. Huebsch, Inc., renewed 1950 by Ivor S. Roberts. Copyright © 1930 by Viking Penguin, Inc., renewed copyright © 1958 by Ivor S. Roberts. Used by permission of Viking Penguin, a division of Penguin Putnam Inc.

Carl Sandburg: Excerpt from "Timesweep," in *Honey and Salt*. Copyright © 1963 by Carl Sandburg and renewed 1991 by Margaret Sandburg, Helga Sandburg Crile, and Janet Sandburg, reprinted by permission of Harcourt, Inc.

Monica Shannon: "My Opinion," from *Goose Grass Rhymes*, by Monica Shannon. Copyright © 1930 by Doubleday, a division of Bantam Doubleday Dell Publishing Group, Inc. Used by permission of Doubleday, a division of Random House, Inc.

Kaye Starbird: "Sparrows," by Kaye Starbird. Reprinted with the permission of Simon & Schuster Books for Young Readers, an imprint of Simon & Schuster's Children's Publishing Division, from *The Covered Bridge House*, by Kaye Starbird. Copyright © 1979 Kaye Starbird Jennison.

Arnold Sundgaard: "The Duck-Billed Platypus" and "The Elephant," by Arnold Sundgaard. Copyright © 1989 by Arnold Sundgaard. Reprinted by permission of the author.

James S. Tippett: "The Red Hen," from *Crickety Cricket! The Best Loved Poems of James S. Tippet*. Copyright 1933, copyright renewed © 1973 by Martha K. Tippet. Used by permission of HarperCollins Publishers.

Judith Viorst: "Mother Doesn't Want a Dog." Reprinted with the permission of Atheneum Books for Young Readers, an imprint of Simon & Schuster Children's Publishing Division, from *If I Were in Charge of the World and Other Worries*, by Judith Viorst. Copyright © 1981 by Judith Viorst.

Valerie Worth: "tiger," from *Small Poems Again*, by Valerie Worth. Copyright © 1975, 1986 by Valerie Worth. Reprinted by permission of Farrar, Straus and Giroux, LLC.

Yaku: "Haiku," from *Birds, Frogs, and Moonlight*, translated by Sylvia Cassedy and Kunihiro Suetake. Copyright © 1967 by Doubleday & Co. Reprinted by permission of Ellen Cassedy.

Eric Carle prepares his own colored tissue papers. Different textures are achieved by using various brushes to splash, spatter, and finger paint acrylic paints onto thin tissue papers. These colored tissue papers then become his palette. They are cut or torn into shapes as needed and are glued onto white illustration board. Some areas of his design, however, are painted directly on the board before the bits of tissue paper are applied to make the collage illustration.

WORLD OF ERIC CARLE
An imprint of Penguin Random House LLC, New York

First published in the United States of America by Philomel Books, an imprint of Penguin Random House LLC, New York, 1989

Published by Puffin Books, 1999

This edition published in the United States of America by World of Eric Carle, an imprint of Penguin Random House LLC, New York, 2020

Illustrations copyright © 1989 by Penguin Random House LLC

ERIC CARLE's name and signature logotype and the World of Eric Carle logo are trademarks and THE VERY HUNGRY CATERPILLAR is a registered trademark of Penguin Random House LLC.

To find out more about Eric Carle and his books, please visit eric-carle.com.

To learn about The Eric Carle Museum of Picture Book Art, please visit carlemuseum.org.

Visit us online at penguinrandomhouse.com.

Library of Congress Control Number: 88031646

Manufactured in China

ISBN 9780698118553   40 39 38

The publisher does not have any control over and does not assume any responsibility for author or third-party websites or their content.

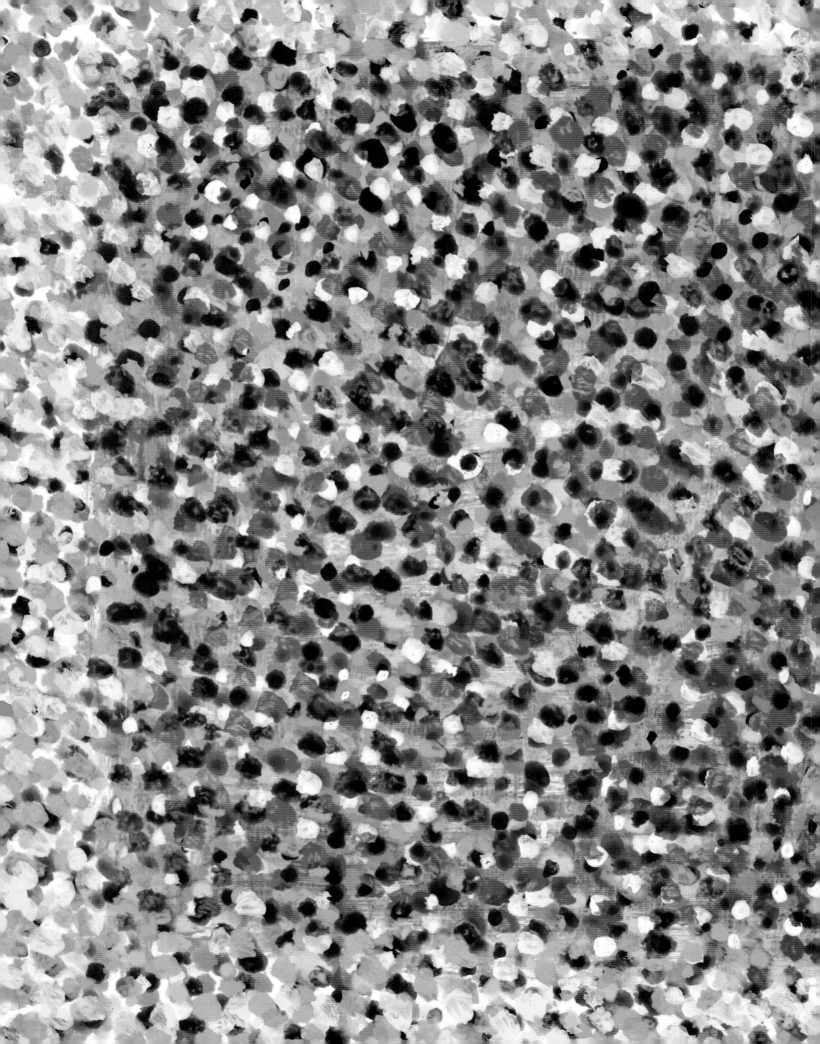

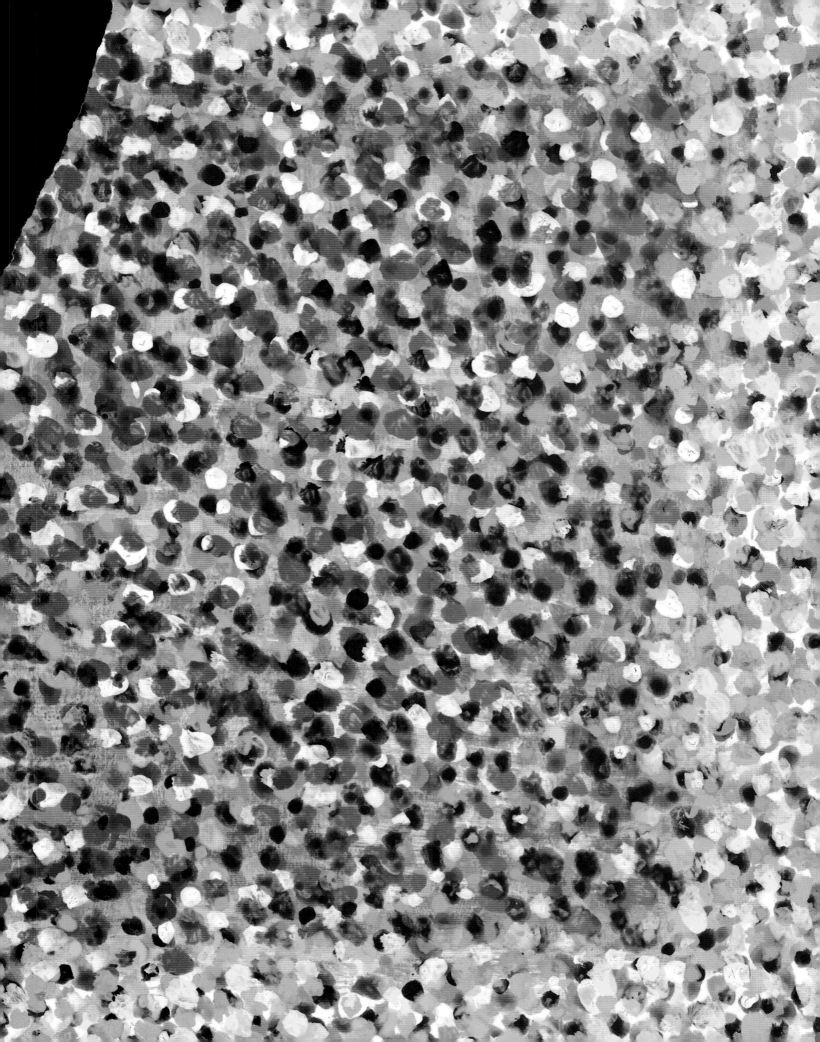

Eric Carle's distinctive, vibrantly colored collage art holds a special place in the world of children's books. Formerly a graphic designer for *The New York Times*, as well as an art director for an advertising agency, Carle has been writing and illustrating children's books for more than thirty years. His enormously popular books include his classic, *The Very Hungry Caterpillar*, which has sold millions of copies worldwide, as well as *The Very Busy Spider*, *1, 2, 3 to the Zoo*, *The Very Clumsy Click Beetle*, and many more.

Laura Whipple, who collected the poems for this anthology, is an elementary school media specialist in New Jersey. She graduated from the Rutgers University Graduate School of Communication, Information and Library Studies, and has worked with young children and poetry for many years. One of her professional goals is to help students learn to love the language of poetry as much as she does.